Cowboy Dad Companion Workbook

Cowboy Dad Companion Workbook
Guided Writing for Adult Children of Alcoholics

MELISSA BROUGHTON M.ED.

© 2017 Melissa Broughton M.Ed.
All rights reserved.

ISBN-13: 9781975751692
ISBN-10: 1975751698

Preface

Whether it was a gift from someone or a present to yourself, congratulations on taking the steps to better understanding yourself and your parent with alcoholism. By working through this Companion Workbook, you will greatly benefit in so many lovely ways and consequently so will the people around you. I decided to write this Companion Workbook for a few reasons. Writing *Cowboy Dad* was one of the most healing things I did for myself after my Dad passed away and the more I talked with other people about their "cowboys" at book signings, class visits and via email, the more I realized that other Adult Children of Alcoholics can move toward healing through writing too. This further understanding and awareness of one's self and their parent leads to insightful, critically thoughtful and deep questions. Meaningful, non-shaming conversations are had and I believe, ultimately, less stigma and more understanding of mental health and addiction are achieved. I'm so grateful that readers get to "meet" my Cowboy Dad and that his life story has and will continue to help others.

Introduction

Hello, my dear, fellow ACAs (Adult Children of an Alcoholic). We don't know each other, but we have a lot in common. As ACAs, we have an ability to sense things (potential trouble and conflict, others' feelings), adapt quickly and our resiliency is pretty amazing. We weren't born with these special gifts, we earned them unconsciously as children. We lived in chaos and inconsistent environments at various levels and times and we survived it by taking on certain psychological roles. Did you think everyone had these strengths? This may or may not be new insight for you, but either way, reading *Cowboy Dad* and working through the Companion Workbook will help you further understand why you act and think a certain way at work, in relationships and just in life overall. This awareness will bring about understanding, awareness and healing too. We had a challenging upbringing; let's acknowledge the heartache and confusion, but use the lessons and experiences to reveal our resiliency. And let's try a hand at forgiveness and peace; let's see our parent for who they are/were and separate that from the disease they are battling (or battled). This perspective doesn't excuse bad behavior and decisions, but it certainly helps us better comprehend our life with our parent, the person and the alcoholic.

Instructions for this Companion Workbook

1. Be sure to have your copy of *Cowboy Dad* as you go through the Workbook as it corresponds with each chapter. Read each chapter, then do the corresponding chapter in the Workbook.

2. Don't skip chapters or read ahead before you finish the prompts and writing for each chapter as you go along.
3. Make sure to find a quiet space to read, reflect and write/journal. Also, allow enough time so that you are not rushed. This is your time and healing gift to yourself.

Now that you have your books – Cowboy Dad and the Companion Workbook, time and a quiet space:

4. Read the chapter. This should resonate with your own experiences and prompt thoughts and memories.
5. When we are stressed or delving into something that could bring stress, we tighten up and even have shortened breath. Remember to BREATHE.
6. Read the Write-to-Heal prompt.
7. Breathe. Close your eyes and slowly start to think about the reading, the prompt and be aware of what thoughts and feelings come up for you that you will be writing about.
8. Write/Journal.

2 Helpful Reflection and Writing Tips:

1. Do not worry about spelling, grammar, perfection, etc. Write whatever you want. It's confidential (unless you decide to share it). Write what comes to mind even if it makes no sense (because it probably makes total sense).
2. Use your senses when you are recalling and writing about a memory. Senses: Sight, sound, taste, smell, touch. There are good examples of this in each chapter; the opening paragraph is a good example.

Considerations and Suggestions:

1. As you work through the reading and workbook, the work will be revealing, healing, nurturing and perhaps also emotionally challenging. You might consider finding a therapist to meet with once a week to debrief and discuss the feelings and memories that come up. This will support your healing.
2. Group therapy has been proven (and I can attest!) to be very insightful, encouraging and healing. Ask a therapist or research online for group therapy for Adult Children of Alcoholics and/or attend an Al-Anon or Adult Children of Alcoholics meeting.
3. Perhaps you don't want to do this alone. Ask a few friends who you know have similar backgrounds and ask if they want to do a book study together. Create your own personal, group therapy!

*Please note:

For the purposes of the Companion Workbook, I choose to use the word "parent" or "your person" even sometimes "your cowboy", which in the case of this Workbook, these terms <u>refer to the parent/person who has/had alcoholism</u>.

2 Things to Keep in Mind:

1. This book is about a father and daughter, so I use "parent", but if the person who has alcoholism that you know is your spouse, child, friend, etc., then just replace "parent" with whomever that person is to you.
2. The use of "cowboy" is not meant to offend or assume that all cowboys are alcoholics. Unexpectedly, it has been used as a "safe" word when people want to talk with me about their story and they are finding it difficult to admit or say the word, "alcoholic". Using "cowboy" feels safer to them.

OPTIONAL:

12-Step. This part is designed for those of you who are familiar with, refer to and utilize the 12-Step philosophy whether it be for AA or Al-Anon. This is a language that many people in recovery use, so this step may be helpful to incorporate into your understanding of this material.

One

REFLECTION

The opening paragraph of the book, paints a vivid image of the Cowboy and the scene taking place. Reflect on your "Cowboy", have a mental picture of them and think about the last time you saw them whether it was yesterday or five years ago.

Write-to-Heal Prompts

1. Write about the last time you saw your person. Be as descriptive as possible: When, where, why, how. Remember to include feelings and using your senses, describe the scene.

_____

_____

_____

2. In Chapter 1, it reads, "My tears were confined within the boundaries of my eyelids, red and eager to blink. My nerves felt like a thousand-piece, glass puzzle, vulnerable to the slightest gust. *Stay strong. Focus. Don't cry, I thought.*" Now, write about a time when your actions were not aligned with what you were feeling.

_____

_____

12-Step: Which step could be utilized/reflected upon in situations similar to the scenario in Chapter 1?

#

Reflection

*I*n this chapter, the author sees something/someone that triggers anxiety which prompts contemplation about what she's missing, wondering, struggling over. Reflect on any situation, thing or person that may be a trigger for you in the same way.

Write-to-Heal Prompts

1. Write about your trigger/s. Why do these things (people, places, smells, etc.) trigger you? How do you feel? Is there resolution? How long does it take you to recuperate from these triggers and how do you handle it at inconvenient times (at work, for example)?

_____

_____

_____

_____

_____

_____

_____

_____

_____

_____

12-Step: Which step could be utilized/reflected upon in situations similar to the scenario in Chapter 2?

Three

REFLECTION

Chapter 3 reveals a childhood memory with the alcoholic parent. Reflect on a childhood memory that seems quite vivid and engrained into your mind.

Write-to-Heal Prompts

1. Write about this childhood memory. Be as descriptive as possible: When, where, why, how. Remember to include feelings and use your senses to describe the scene.

_____

_____

_____

_____

_____

2. Dinner time for our family was …

12-Step: Which step could be utilized/reflected upon in situations similar to the scenario in Chapter 3?

Four

REFLECTION

*C*hapter 4 shares the story of how the author "escaped" and took a leap of faith to a faraway and new place. Reflect on a time when you ran away, escaped, and/or took a leap of faith. Perhaps you didn't actually leave or move, but you did something else that was a leap or an escape.

Write-to-Heal Prompts

1. Write about your "adventure". Be as descriptive as possible: When, where, why, how. Remember to include feelings and using your senses, describe the scene. Were you running away from or towards something?

_____

_____

_____

2. During this time in my life (my escape), I …

3. The last time I did something for the first time was …

_____

_____

_____

_____

_____

_____

_____

_____

12-Step: Which step could be utilized/reflected upon in situations similar to the scenario in Chapter 4?

Five

REFLECTION

*T*he last section of this chapter reveals the family history of alcoholism. Reflect on your own family history of addiction.

Write-to-Heal Prompts

1. Write about the history of addiction in your family. Either draw a family tree and/or write about a specific incident that you can remember. Be as descriptive as possible: When, where, why, how. Remember to include feelings and using your senses, describe the scene.

_____

_____

_____

_____

2. When I was a child, I really loved …

12-Step: Which step/s could be utilized/reflected upon in situations similar to the scenarios in Chapter 5?

Six

REFLECTION

In Chapter 6 the author shares about times when she felt like a grown up as a child as well as feeling rebellious. Can you relate to this?

Write-to-Heal Prompts

1. Even though I was just a kid, I felt all grown up when …

   _____

   _____

   _____

   _____

   _____

2. If someone could put a drinking glass against the wall to hear the arguments about drinking in your personal situation, what might they hear?

3. As a child or teen, were you asked for advice by your parent? Write about that: When, why, what, how did it make you feel?

_____

_____

_____

_____

_____

_____

_____

_____

4. I felt rebellious when …

_____

_____

_____

_____

5. Did your person ever give you "trinket apologies"?

12-Step: Which step could be utilized/reflected upon in situations similar to the scenario in Chapter 6?

Seven

REFLECTION

Chapter 7 reveals the high school boyfriend. Remember your high school sweetheart? At the same time, the author reveals times when, aside from being a high schooler with a boyfriend, she had to be like an adult when her father was drunk. Can you relate?

Write-to-Heal Prompts

1. Write about your high school crush and/or boyfriend or girlfriend. Were they a positive or negative influence? Be as descriptive as possible: When, where, why, how. Remember to include feelings and using your senses, describe the scene.

_____

_____

_____

2. I realized I had no control over my family when …

3. Write about a time when you had to take over a situation because your parent was incapable due to being intoxicated.

_____

_____

_____

_____

_____

_____

_____

_____

_____

12-Step: Which step could be utilized/reflected upon in situations similar to the scenario in Chapter 7?

Eight

REFLECTION

In Chapter 8, the author writes about leaving home to go to college. She was relieved and enthusiastic about escaping the certain aspects of alcoholism. Not too long after leaving home, she got married despite having a gut feeling she shouldn't get hitched. Do you relate to this chapter?

Write-to-Heal Prompts

1. How did you feel when you left home for the first time (to go to college or for a job, etc)? Be as descriptive as possible: When, where, why, how. Remember to include feelings and using your senses, describe the scene.

_____

_____

_____

2. Have you ever "rescued" the alcoholic parent from a situation because they were intoxicated?

3. The author felt reluctance about getting married. Has there been a time when you had reluctance, but moved forward anyway?

12-Step: Which step could be utilized/reflected upon in situations similar to the scenario in Chapter 8?

Nine

Reflection

Despite being away from home, the author finds herself still involved and helping the alcoholic parent. How and why do you relate to Chapter 9?

Write-to-Heal Prompts

1. Did you find yourself continuing to help the alcoholic parent even though you left home?

_____

_____

_____

_____

_____

2. Did your relations with your alcoholic parent have an impact on other relationships in your life?

3. The author writes about having a "…well of hope in her heart." Did or do you continue to have hope for your parent?

_____

_____

_____

_____

_____

_____

_____

_____

12-Step: Which step could be utilized/reflected upon in situations similar to the scenario in Chapter 9?

Ten

REFLECTION

When we lie or cover for the alcoholic, it feels and seems like we're doing the right thing and at the same time there's a conflicting feeling of shame. The author touches on this in this chapter. How and why did you relate to Chapter 10?

Write-to-Heal Prompts

1. Write about time when you lied/covered for your parent. Be as descriptive as possible: When, where, why, how. Remember to include feelings and using your senses, describe the scene.

_____

_____

_____

2. Write about a time when you were ashamed of your parent and how you tried to hide it.

3. I finally hit rock bottom emotionally when …

12-Step: Which step could be utilized/reflected upon in situations similar to the scenario in Chapter 10?

Eleven

Reflection

The author writes about visiting her childhood home; she seems to have such a deep connection to the Ranch. And "Home" can mean different things. How and why do you relate to Chapter 11?

Write-to-Heal Prompts

1. Have you ever revisited your childhood home? Be as descriptive as possible: When, where, why, how. Remember to include feelings and using your senses, describe the scene.

_____

_____

_____

_____

2. Going home makes me feel …

3. If you have negative childhood memories, is your perspective on them any different now that you're an adult?

_____

_____

_____

_____

_____

_____

_____

_____

_____

12-Step: Which step could be utilized/reflected upon in situations similar to the scenario in Chapter 11?

Twelve

REFLECTION

The author shares her frustration comically and candidly regarding buying a card for her father. Can you relate to these feelings and frustrations in Chapter 12?

Write-to-Heal Prompts

1. Like the author, write a card and describe the cover of a card to your parent from the perspective of: Child, teen, adult.

_____

_____

_____

_____

2. Father's Day and/or Mother's Day make me feel …

12-Step: Which step could be utilized/reflected upon in situations similar to the scenario in Chapter 12?

Thirteen

Reflection

The author writes several examples in the book that show the contrast between the person and the disease. Can you separate the person from the disease? How and why do you relate to Chapter 13?

Write-to-Heal Prompts

1. Think about a positive memory that reveals the contrast between the healthy part of the relationship and the disease.

_____

_____

_____

_____

2. Have you ever found yourself guarding your heart by holding back feelings?

3. Think of a happy memory – one where your parent was sober and they helped you and/or gave you advice.

_____

_____

_____

_____

_____

_____

_____

_____

_____

12-Step: Which step could be utilized/reflected upon in situations similar to the scenario in Chapter 13?

Fourteen

REFLECTION

Chapter 14 touches on a few concepts around Adult Children of Alcoholics being more sensitive and aware of their surroundings. This has an impact on communication, and relationships to say the least. How and why do you relate to Chapter 14?

Write-to-Heal Prompts

1. As an ACA, do you feel that you have "superhero" intuition?

_____

_____

_____

_____

2. Are or were you able to speak with your parent candidly about their disease?

3. How has being an ACA affected your romantic relationships?

4. The truth is …

_____

_____

_____

_____

_____

12-Step: Which step could be utilized/reflected upon in situations similar to the scenario in Chapter 14?

Fifteen

REFLECTION

A therapist by the name of John Bradshaw talked about Toxic Shame. Chapter 15 touches on how this shame can devastate the alcoholic and the family. How do you relate to this concept?

Write-to-Heal Prompts

1. Do you know what "toxic shame" is? Have you noticed your parent experiencing toxic shame?

___

___

___

___

2. Re-read the paragraph: *The genuine promises, good intentions and a sincere desire to be and do better --these thoughts, words and actions of an addict are heart-breaking to, yes, the people around them, but also for the person with the addiction. These are not empty promises or vindictive actions; they are true desires and when their disease lets others and themselves down (again and again), it's devastating to their spirit. And so, the addiction wins again with another hit.* How can you relate this idea from the book to your parent?

_____

_____

_____

_____

12-Step: Which step could be utilized/reflected upon in situations similar to the scenario in Chapter 15?

Sixteen

REFLECTION

The blessing of true friendship and the reality of life and death -- this is an emotional chapter to read. Take a few deep breaths.

Write-to-Heal Prompts

1. Write about your best friend

_____

_____

_____

_____

2. How have your friendships changed through the years?

12-Step: Which step could be utilized/reflected upon in situations similar to the scenario in Chapter 16?

Seventeen

REFLECTION

The author remembers and then writes a very detailed description of her Cowboy. This is very healing. Can you do this?

Write-to-Heal Prompts

1. Write about your parent, describing both their physical characteristics and their personality and character.

_____

_____

_____

_____

_____

Cowboy Dad Companion Workbook

Eighteen

REFLECTION

In Chapter 18 and many other chapters, the author describes being codependent and how she may feel comfort in being codependent and even comfort in times of chaos. How and why do you relate to Chapter 18?

Write-to-Heal Prompts

1. I feel the urge to protect my parent when …

_____

_____

_____

_____

2. Have you witnessed your parent express emotions when they are sober?

3. Do you tend to feel more comfortable in chaotic or calm situations?

_____
_____
_____
_____
_____
_____
_____
_____
_____

12-Step: Which step could be utilized/reflected upon in situations similar to the scenario in Chapter 18?

Nineteen

REFLECTION

At the beginning of this chapter, the author summarizes the move from Colorado, to Arizona and back to Colorado again, all due to the alcoholic dynamics of running away and ultimately losing jobs. Inconsistency like this, in the home – not knowing what to expect, parent losing a job, etc. can wreak havoc on childhood development. On the flip side, the author then gives examples of how her father was loving and helpful when she was young. How and why do you relate to Chapter 19?

Write-to-Heal Prompts

1. Did your parent lose a job due to drinking? How did that make you feel?

_____

_____

_____

Melissa Broughton M.Ed.

2. Did your parent ever gain something back because of his ability to be charismatic and charming?

3. Write about another happy memory when your parent was sober and loving and supportive in some way.

12-Step: Which step could be utilized/reflected upon in situations similar to the scenario in Chapter 19?

Reflection

This chapter shares the ups and downs of belief in a Higher Power and it shows love, alcoholism and a dying way of life just as the subtitle of this books summarizes. How do you relate to Chapter 20?

Write-to-Heal Prompts

1. Have you ever prayed to, begged or negotiated with God about your parent?

_____

_____

_____

_____

2. Have you ever lost or gained faith in God or a Higher Power?

3. I prayed for …

_____

_____

_____

_____

_____

_____

_____

_____

4. Have you ever been in denial about your parent's disease?

_____

_____

_____

5. I felt defeated when …

12-Step: Which step could be utilized/reflected upon in situations similar to the scenario in Chapter 20?

Reflection

In Chapter 21, the author comes to realize that she needs to focus on healing and her life. That's easier said than done when you're used to being worried and codependent with someone who is no longer living. How do you relate to Chapter 21?

Write-to-Heal Prompts

1. Has there been a time when you realized that you needed to focus on yourself and not your parent?

_____

_____

_____

_____

_____

_____

_____

_____

_____

_____

12-Step: Which step could be utilized/reflected upon in situations similar to the scenario in Chapter 21?

Twenty-Two

REFLECTION

Understanding the family roles was an ah-ha moment for the author in understanding her way of thinking and living her life. These family roles were identified by family therapist, Sharon Wegscheider-Cruse; she identified these roles as "The Family Trap". Hopefully this information will give you the same insight as it did the author. *Additional information and other characteristics of Adult Children of Alcoholics can be found at: www.adultchildren.org and www.al-anon.org.

Write-to-Heal Prompts

1. As the author writes about in this chapter, there are "family survival roles" that each family member in an alcoholic home, take on to essentially "survive" the chaos. These roles are: Alcoholic, Enabler, Hero (model child), Scapegoat (problem child), Lost Child (demands little, receives little) and Mascot (class/family clown). The non-alcoholic spouse is usually the Enabler. Write about your role – how and why? How has this had a positive and negative impact on your character?

12-Step: Which step could be utilized/reflected upon in situations similar to the scenario in Chapter 22?

Reflection

In this chapter, we do see how positive things can come out of bad experiences. How and why do you relate to Chapter 23?

Write-to-Heal Prompts

1. The author says she received "grace through alcoholism". Have you received any grace through your parent's disease, life or death?

_____
_____
_____
_____
_____

2. The author writes, "The effect of alcoholism sometimes disguises the true character of the person struggling with the addiction." Give your own example of this.

3. Has growing up with an alcoholic or being an ACA affected your spiritual life in some way?

_____
_____
_____
_____
_____
_____
_____
_____
_____
_____

12-Step: Which step could be utilized/reflected upon in situations similar to the scenario in Chapter 23?

Twenty-Four

REFLECTION

In this chapter, the author realizes how she has grown and has a deeper understanding of her Cowboy. How and why do you relate to Chapter 24?

Write-to-Heal Prompts

1. Through these reflections and writing exercises, do you view your "Cowboy" differently?

___

___

___

___

___

_____

_____

_____

_____

_____

12-Step: Which step could be utilized/reflected upon in situations similar to the scenario in Chapter 24?

Reflection

*I*n the end of this life, or the lives of the people we love, we have: Wisdom, lessons, and memories. Chapter 25 reveals reflection and healing in a memory of being on the ranch with her Dad. Do you have a memory that you want to write about?

Write-to-Heal Prompts

1. As an ACA, you have survived many challenges. Write about how this experience has shaped your character. Write about your resiliency my dear fellow ACA.

_____

_____

_____

Melissa Broughton M.Ed.

Additional Writing Prompts

- After reading this book …
- Now I understand that …
- If you only knew that …
- If only …
- The truth is …
- Alcoholism is …
- I know that no matter what …
- Sometimes I wonder …
- You'll never believe this, but …
- I will never …
- I felt defeated when …
- I'm stronger because …
- I'm wiser because …

Additional Discussion and Writing Prompts for Self or Support Group

- What would be the title of your memoir?

- There are several divine interventions in this story. Find them and discuss them and your own experiences with divine intervention.

- There are several examples of codependency in this story. Find them and discuss them and your own experiences with codependency. More specifically, how do you think being co-dependent has <u>not</u> been beneficial to you, but also, do you think being co-dependent has/had any benefits?

- There are lots of examples showing the contrast between the person and the disease (the person when they have been drinking). Find them and discuss them and your own examples of the person verses the disease.

Further notes, thoughts and reflections

Made in the USA
Middletown, DE
04 June 2021